Arctic Fox on the Move

Katie Peters

GRL Consultant Diane Craig, Certified Literacy Specialist

Lerner Publications ◆ Minneapolis

Lerner Publications
An imprint of Lerner Publishing Group, Inc.
241 First Avenue North
Minneapolis, MN 55401 USA

For reading levels and more information, look up this title at www.lernerbooks.com.

Main body text set in Memphis Pro 24/39
Typeface provided by Linotype.

Photo Acknowledgments
The images in this book are used with the permission of: © Eric Isselee/Shutterstock Images, p. 3; © Page Chichester/iStockphoto, pp. 4–5, 16 (center); © Menno Schaefer/Adobe Stock, pp. 6–7, 16 (left); © EEI_Tony/iStockphoto, pp. 8–9; © Schaef1/M. Schaefer-Fotografie, pp. 10–11; © Wirestock/iStockphoto, pp. 12–13; © Chansak Joe/iStockphoto, pp. 14–15, 16 (right).

Front cover: © Alexey_Seafarer/iStockphoto

Library of Congress Cataloging-in-Publication Data

Names: Peters, Katie, author.
Title: Arctic fox on the move / Katie Peters.
Description: Minneapolis : Lerner Publications, [2025] | Series: Let's look at polar animals (pull ahead readers - nonfiction) | Includes index. | Audience: Ages 4–7 | Audience: Grades K–1 | Summary: "Arctic foxes are busy little creatures. Leveled text and full-color photographs help support learning about these active animals. Pairs with the fiction title, Frosty's Snow Day"—Provided by publisher.
Identifiers: LCCN 2023031817 (print) | LCCN 2023031818 (ebook) | ISBN 9798765626269 (library binding) | ISBN 9798765629291 (paperback) | ISBN 9798765634561 (epub)
Subjects: LCSH: Arctic fox—Juvenile literature.
Classification: LCC QL737.C22 P455 2025 (print) | LCC QL737.C22 (ebook) | DDC 599.775—dc23/eng/20230717

LC record available at https://lccn.loc.gov/2023031817
LC ebook record available at https://lccn.loc.gov/2023031818

Manufactured in the United States of America
1 – CG – 7/15/24

Table of Contents

Arctic Fox on the Move

The fox runs.

The fox jumps.

The fox digs.

The fox hunts.

The fox eats.

The fox sleeps.

Did You See It?

jumps

runs

sleeps

Index